100 AMAZING FACTS ABOUT AUSTRALIA

Content

"In the skies over Australia, I saw it: a world strangely elusive and beautiful, fierce yet fragile."

— David Malouf

Introduction

As someone who holds this book in your hands, you are no doubt driven by an insatiable curiosity and a burning desire to discover the wonders of a continent as vast as it is enigmatic: Australia. Maybe you've already been charmed by its varied landscapes, from the Great Barrier Reef to the wild outback, or maybe you only have a vague idea of what this far-flung land has to offer. Either way, get ready for a fascinating journey through 100 mind-blowing facts that paint Australia in a new light.

Australia is not just a land of kangaroos and koalas. It has a rich history, a diverse culture and an unrivalled natural heritage. As you walk through these pages, you'll be immersed in captivating tales, from centuries-old Aboriginal myths to modern exploits, to the unique flora and fauna that make this continent a true treasure trove of biodiversity.

So, let your curiosity guide you and embark on this adventure in the heart of Australia. You will discover amazing facts, touching stories and wonders that are sure to surprise you. Are you ready? Open your eyes wide, Australia awaits you with its secrets and legends.

Marc Dresgui

Fact 1 - 10 out of the 15 most dangerous snakes

Are you afraid of snakes? If so, Australia has a few surprises in store for you! Indeed, this remote continent is home to 10 of the 15 most venomous snakes in the world. Impressive, isn't it? But don't worry, most of them prefer to stay away from humans.

The Taipan from the inside is a good example. Considered the most venomous snake on the planet, it holds venom so potent that a single bite could kill many adults. Fortunately, it is rather shy and usually avoids inhabited areas. You also have the Eastern Brown Snake, which, despite its medium size, holds fearsome venom.

But it's not all bad news! In fact, very few people in Australia are bitten by these venomous creatures, and even fewer die from them, thanks to effective antivenom treatments and awareness of the danger. So, if you're visiting Australia, admire these fascinating creatures from afar and respect their space. They are an integral part of this country's unique ecosystem.

Fact 2 - Kangaroos: exclusive to Australia!

When you think of Australia, what is one of the first animals that comes to mind? The kangaroo, of course! These leaping creatures are iconic to Australia and, you know what? They are not found in the wild anywhere else in the world!

Imagine a vast, open landscape with free-jumping kangaroos is a common sight in Australia. In fact, the kangaroo population is so large that it often exceeds the number of humans on the continent! It is not uncommon for Australians to see these marsupials in their backyards or on the side of the road.

But the kangaroo isn't just famous for its jumps. Have you ever heard of the kangaroo pouch? It's a cozy place where kangaroo moms carry their young, called joeys, for several months after they are born.

So, next time you think of Australia, remember those amazing jumping animals. They are an essential part of Australia's identity and continue to amaze people around the world with their unique demeanor and iconic allure.

Fact 3 – Koalas: Born and Raised Here

Ah, koalas! With their round faces, bushy ears, and love for eucalyptus trees, they are among the most adored creatures in the world. Did you know that these small marsupials are native to Australia and only live in the wild there?

These furballs nimbly climb eucalyptus trees, their main source of food. In fact, they are so specialized that they depend almost exclusively on certain varieties of these trees. Thanks to a slow metabolism, they can spend up to 20 hours a day sleeping, often perched high up in a tree!

But the koala isn't just a cute face. It plays a crucial role in the Australian ecosystem. By feeding on eucalyptus leaves, they help regulate the growth of these trees and maintain the balance of their environment.

If you're lucky enough to visit Australia one day, keep your eyes peeled and look towards the trees. If you're lucky, you might spot a koala taking a nap or a quiet snack, reminding everyone of their special place in this faraway land.

Fact 4 - More wild camels than anywhere else

When you think of camels, you probably picture sandy deserts in the Middle East, right? But did you know that Australia is home to the largest population of wild camels in the world? It's true, and it's an amazing fact!

Originally, camels were introduced to Australia in the 19th century to help with construction work and transport through arid regions. But once roads and railways were built, many of these camels were released back into the wild. They adapted so well to the conditions of the Australian desert that they thrived.

Today, their number is estimated at more than one million in the desert regions of the country. While walking through the outback, it is not uncommon to come across a herd of wild camels crossing the landscape.

This is one of the many surprises Australia has to offer. A continent known for its kangaroos and koalas is also home to the largest population of wild camels. Who would have thought?

Fact 5 - Wombats: cube-shaped poop?

Wombats are funny little Australian creatures. But did you know that these nocturnal animals have a truly amazing characteristic? They produce excrement... cube-shaped! Yes, you read that right: cubes!

These hardy marsupials spend much of their time tunneling into the ground, but that's not where the cube magic happens. The unique shape of their droppings is actually a clever way to mark their territory. Because they are cubic, the droppings don't roll easily, allowing wombats to leave a clear message for others: "This is my territory!"

Nature is full of surprises, isn't it? But why cubes? Scientists believe that this shape also helps retain the moisture of the feces, which is essential in an often dry environment.

The next time you hear about wombats, you'll remember this fun fact. This is further proof that Australia is truly a place full of wonders and curiosities!

Fact 6 - The Funnel Web Spider

Australia is famous for its unique wildlife, but some of its creatures are a bit scarier than others. Have you ever heard of the funnel web spider? It is recognized as one of the most dangerous spiders in the world, so beware!

These spiders don't spin hanging webs like many others. Instead, they dig funnel-shaped tunnels in the ground from which they can surprise their prey. If you're walking in Australia and see a cone-shaped hole in the ground, it's likely that a funnel-web spider is lurking inside.

But it's not just their hunting technique that's remarkable. Their venom is extremely potent and can be dangerous to humans. Fortunately, antivenoms are available, and fatal bites are rare these days.

So, if you find yourself in Australia, be careful where you step and always be aware of your surroundings. Australia is a fascinating place, but it's always good to know the potential dangers lurking there.

Fact 7 – The Strange and Unique Platypuses

The platypus is arguably one of the strangest animals you can imagine. With a duck-like beak, otter body, and beaver feet, this animal appears to be a mix of several different creatures. But believe it or not, it's real and it's native to Australia!

These animals live near rivers and lakes, where they spend their time swimming in search of food. But what's even more amazing is that platypuses are one of the few mammals to lay eggs. Yes, you heard right, eggs!

But wait, there's more. Males have a sting on their hind legs that can release venom. Although this venom is not usually fatal to humans, it can cause severe pain.

So, the next time you think of Australia, remember that this continent is not just the land of kangaroos and koalas. It's also home to the platypus, one of the most incredible creatures on the planet!

Fact 8 – Tasmanian Devils: Not Just a Cartoon!

When we hear "Tasmanian Devil", we often think of the swirling, noisy character from cartoons. But did you know that the real Tasmanian devils are fascinating creatures that live in Australia, more precisely on the island of Tasmania?

These small, carnivorous marsupials are about the size of a small dog and have coarse, black fur. But don't be fooled by their small size. When agitated or threatened, they can emit very loud grunts and screams, hence their evocative name "devil".

An interesting fact is that, despite their somewhat creepy appearance, Tasmanian devils play a crucial role in their ecosystem by cleaning up the carcasses of dead animals. This helps keep their habitat clean and healthy.

So, the next time you see the Tasmanian Devil on TV, remember that these creatures really do exist and they are of major importance to the environment in Australia. They are much more than just cartoon characters!

Fact 9 - Emus, the Runner Birds

Have you ever heard of emu? It is the second largest bird in the world, second only to the African ostrich! Native to Australia, the emu is really impressive with its height that can reach almost 2 meters.

The emu is a runner bird, which means it does not fly. Instead, it has long, powerful legs that allow it to run at speeds of up to 50 km/h! If you tried to chase after him, he would quickly outrun you.

Another fascinating aspect of emus is their role in raising their young. Did you know that it is the males who incubate the eggs and take care of the chicks once they hatch? For nearly eight weeks, the male sits on the eggs, only getting up to drink.

So, when you think of Australia, don't forget the emu, this incredible bird that roams the vast expanses of the country. This is another one of the many unique wonders that can be found on this amazing continent!

Fact 10 - Possums, Our Nocturnal Neighbors

Ah, possums! These small, thick-furred creatures are one of Australia's nocturnal wonders. If you're walking around Australia for a night, it's very likely that you'll come across a possum perched on a tree or silently exploring the surrounding area.

Contrary to what their name might suggest, Australian possums are not identical to the possums that can be found in America. They are actually part of a completely different family of animals. These marsupials are usually smaller and have soft, shiny fur.

A fun fact about possums is their diet. They love leaves, fruits, and flowers, but they're also known to be a bit greedy! Some Australians say that possums sometimes come and steal fruit from their gardens.

So, even though they're nocturnal and a bit inconspicuous, possums play a valuable role in the Australian ecosystem. These little marsupials add a touch of magic to the nights of the country-continent!

Fact 11 - Miniature Continent, Huge Nation

Did you know that Australia is a bit of a geographical enigma? It is the only place on Earth that is both a country and a continent. But be careful! Even though it's the smallest continent, as a country, Australia is gigantic.

Imagine a country almost as big as the continental United States, but with a smaller population than the state of California. This gives Australia vast wilderness and breathtaking landscapes, such as the Red Desert of Central and the rainforests of Queensland.

Speaking of deserts, did you know that Australia is home to one of the driest places on earth? This is the Simpson Desert, where it may not rain for years. But conversely, the country also has very humid regions, such as the Daintree Rainforest.

In short, Australia is a country of contrasts, with a size that defies imagination. From arid desert to golden beaches, it is a land of diversity and vastness.

Fact 12 - Tasmania's 408 km/h winds

Can you imagine being outside when the wind is blowing at 408 km/h? It's almost inconceivable, isn't it? And yet, in Tasmania, an island south of Australia, this incredible weather phenomenon happened!

The place in question is called Maatsuyker Island. It was on this remote island that instruments recorded this breathtaking speed, making this wind one of the fastest ever measured on Earth. To give you an idea, that's almost three times the wind speed of a typical tornado!

These extreme winds are the result of particular weather conditions, combined with the island's unique geography. Winds can pick up significantly as they pass through narrow valleys or over steep cliffs, as is the case at Maatsuyker Island.

So, the next time you're complaining about a windy day, think of Tasmania and its amazing winds! This is further proof that Australia is a land of records and impressive natural phenomena.

Fact 13 - From Deserts to Tropical Beaches

When you think of Australia, what image comes to mind? Kangaroos leaping through an arid desert? Or maybe surfers riding the waves on beautiful golden beaches? The truth is, Australia has both, and so much more!

In its vast interior, you'll find the "Red Centre", where deserts like the Simpson Desert offer landscapes of wild and austere beauty. The red and orange hues of the dunes and rocks are a sight to behold, especially at sunrise or sunset. But be careful, it's very hot!

Then, as you move to the coasts, you'll be amazed by breathtaking tropical beaches. Places like the Gold Coast or Byron Bay are paradises for beachgoers, with their fine sand, turquoise waters and laid-back vibe.

At the end of the day, Australia is a land of contrasts, where natural beauty is revealed in many forms. From the dry and scorching heart of the country to the refreshing shores, there's always something amazing to discover!

Fact 14 - Five Different Climates

Have you ever dreamed of traveling across multiple continents in one country? In Australia, this is possible thanks to its five distinct climate zones! This means that you can experience very different weather conditions depending on where you are.

Start with the tropical north with an equatorial climate. Here, in places like Cairns or Darwin, you'll have seasons marked by heavy rain or drier, but still warm, weather. Imagine walking through a tropical rainforest and then cooling off under a waterfall!

Descend a little further south, and you'll discover a desert climate in places like Alice Springs. The sky is almost always clear, but the sun can be unforgiving during the day. Nights, on the other hand, can be chilly.

On the east and west coasts, the climate is temperate, perfect for lounging on the beaches or hiking. And if you like coolness, southern regions like Melbourne have an oceanic climate, with cooler winters.

In short, no matter where you are in Australia, the weather always offers you something new to discover!

Fact 15 - Uluru: The Sacred Giant Rock

Imagine yourself in front of a huge red rock, standing majestically in the middle of a desert landscape. This is Uluru, also known as Ayers Rock, one of Australia's most iconic symbols. Its presence in the Northern Territory desert is so imposing that it seems almost unearthly.

But Uluru isn't just remarkable for its size or colour. It holds deep spiritual significance for the local Aboriginal people, the Anangu. For them, this rock is sacred, a place of ceremonies and ancestral legends. Walking around, you can even spot cave paintings, witnesses to these ancient stories.

At dawn or dusk, the spectacle is even more impressive. The changing light causes the colour of Uluru to vary from a deep red to a bright orange to a dark purple. It's a magical moment that many come to admire.

So, if you have the chance to visit Australia, don't miss out on this natural and cultural treasure. Respect it like the Anangu do, and it will leave you with an unforgettable memory.

Fact 16 - The Hidden Treasure of Rainforests

Have you ever dreamed of getting lost in a lush forest, where every nook and cranny seems to harbor a new wonder? Australia's rainforests offer you this experience. These dense, humid and vibrant ecosystems are a true hidden treasure of the continent.

In the shade of huge tree ferns and hundred-year-old trees, an exceptional biodiversity flourishes. Did you know, for example, that the cassowary, that impressive bird with a blue shell, is only found in these tropical forests? Its presence is an indicator of the health of this fragile environment.

But that's not all! These forests are also full of crystal clear waterways and spectacular waterfalls. While walking around, you might come across magical places such as the Mossman Gorge or the Millaa Millaa Falls, where the cool water invites you to take a refreshing swim.

So, if you're visiting Australia, take the time to immerse yourself in these havens of peace. Not only will you experience stunning landscapes, but you'll also feel connected to the Earth like never before.

Fact 17 - Fraser Island in Sand

Imagine an island made entirely of sand, where huge dunes border crystal clear lakes. Fraser Island, located off the east coast of Australia, offers you exactly this amazing sight. In fact, it's the largest sand island in the world!

But don't get me wrong, there's more to this island than just its sandy expanses. Despite its composition, abundant vegetation thrives here. Have you ever heard of McKenzie Lake? It is a freshwater lake, pure and clear, surrounded by sand so white that it seems unreal. A real gem in the heart of a sandy island.

Fraser Island is also home to a variety of wildlife. During your walks, you could meet the eyes of a wild dingo or observe humpback whales from the beach during their migration. It is a true paradise for nature lovers.

If you're looking for a unique destination, where nature has sculpted an extraordinary landscape, Fraser Island is the place to be. A must-do Australian experience for any traveller hungry for new adventures!

Fact 18 - The Blue Mountains Show

Have you ever imagined a mountain range that, when seen from a distance, seems bathed in a mystical bluish hue? If not, let me tell you about the Blue Mountains in Australia. Yes, they live up to their name and for good reason!

This blue color is not an illusion. It is due to the evaporation of essential oils produced by eucalyptus trees, which are ubiquitous in these mountains. When sunlight hits these fine suspended particles, blue light is refracted, providing this unique spectacle.

But the Blue Mountains aren't just famous for their hue. They are also home to the famous Three Sisters Rock, an iconic rock formation that you should definitely see. And for the more adventurous, these mountains offer breathtaking hikes and viewpoints.

If you're looking for an incomparable natural experience, a visit to the Blue Mountains is a must. Between eucalyptus forests, impressive canyons and that mesmerizing blue hue, it is a real Australian treasure that awaits you.

Fact 19 - The Naturally Pink Lake

When you think of lakes, what color comes to mind? Blue? Green? How about a pink lake? Yes, you read that right! Australia is home to an exceptional natural phenomenon: Lake Hillier, a salt lake with bright pink waters.

But why is this lake pink? Science suggests that this color comes from a mixture of halophilic bacteria and algae that thrive in the salty conditions of the lake. It is this unique set of organisms that gives Hillier Lake its distinct pink colour.

Located on Middle Island, off the coast of Western Australia, this lake is best enjoyed from above. Aerial views show a stunning contrast between the pink of the lake and the green of the surrounding forests, with the blue ocean as a backdrop.

If you're looking for a truly unique natural spectacle, Lake Hillier is a must-see destination. It's a fascinating reminder of how nature can sometimes overwhelm our imagination.

Fact 20 - Pinnacles, the Mysterious Desert

Have you ever seen a landscape that looks like it came straight out of another planet? The Pinnacles in Western Australia's Nambung National Park offer just that kind of view. Thousands of limestone columns rise from the desert, forming a natural labyrinth that intrigues and fascinates.

The origin of these formations is shrouded in mystery. Some believe that they are the result of the erosion of limestone layers formed thousands of years ago. Over time, wind and water have sculpted these strange structures, which can grow up to four meters in height.

On a visit, you'll be amazed by the contrast between the brilliant blue sky and those mysterious golden-yellow pillars. At sunrise and sunset, the shadow of the Pinnacles creates a striking play of light, a sight not to be missed.

If you're looking for a place that combines mystery, geological history and natural beauty, the Pinnacles are for you. A reminder that Australia is full of natural treasures that defy explanation and imagination.

Fact 21 - 65,000 years of Aboriginal history

Did you know that Australia has one of the oldest living cultures in the world? Aboriginal peoples lived on this vast continent for at least 65,000 years, long before the first Europeans. Their rich cultural heritage is deeply rooted in Australia's history and landscape.

Their connection to the Earth runs deep. The myths of the "Dreamtime" explain the creation of the world and the role of each element of nature. Sacred sites, like Uluru which you may have heard of before, are places of celebration, history and spirituality.

Their artistic know-how is also remarkable. You've probably seen those fascinating and intricate cave paintings or the famous "didgeridoos". These works, far from being mere artistic expressions, tell stories, transmit laws and life lessons.

So, when visiting Australia, take a moment to immerse yourself in this Aboriginal history. It's not just a story of ancient peoples, it's a living and vibrant part of today's Australian identity.

Fact 22 - The very early music of the Didgeridoo

Have you ever heard the deep and mesmerizing sound of the didgeridoo? This seemingly simple instrument is a mainstay of Australian Aboriginal music and has been played for thousands of years. It is carved from eucalyptus trunks naturally hollowed out by termites, which gives it a unique sound.

The game of the didgeridoo does not rely only on the breath: it requires a special technique called "circular breathing". By practicing this technique, musicians can maintain a constant note for a long period of time without interruption, creating a continuous vibration that can be felt as much as heard.

In addition to its musicality, the didgeridoo has a deep cultural significance for Aboriginal peoples. It is often used in sacred ceremonies, accompanying songs and dances. Each instrument tells a story, often painted with motifs depicting totems or stories from the "Dreamtime".

So, the next time you hear this fascinating instrument, remember its ancient heritage and the cultural richness it represents for Australia. It's much more than just an instrument; It's a bridge to an ancient civilization.

Fact 23 - Messages from the Past in Cave Paintings

Have you ever wondered how ancient people communicate their stories and culture? Rock paintings, found throughout Australia, are one of the oldest ways Aboriginal people tell their stories, beliefs and share knowledge. These works of art, which can be up to 40,000 years old, are like a window into the past.

In areas like Kakadu, you can admire paintings depicting animals, hunters, and even scenes from everyday life. Each drawing has a meaning, whether spiritual, didactic, or simply representative of everyday life. These images are much more than just illustrations; They are a way for ancient peoples to pass on their heritage.

These cave paintings are not just historical artifacts. For many Aborigines, they are still alive, linked to places, stories and ancestors. They maintain a strong link with the "Dreamtime", a mythical period when, according to beliefs, the world was shaped.

So, if you ever get the chance to see these paintings, take a moment to connect with their deep history and feel the power of these messages from the past.

Fact 24 - Aboriginal Dream

Have you ever heard of the "Dreamtime"? For the Aboriginal people of Australia, the "Dreamtime" is much more than just a story. It is a sacred moment, a mythical period when ancestral spirits shaped the world and created all the elements that make it up.

The "Dreamtime" encompasses the past, present and future. The stories related to it describe the journeys of ancestral spirits, the creation of mountains, rivers, animals and plants. For example, in some areas, it is told how the rainbow snake carved the landscape as it meandered across the continent.

These stories are not just tales to lull children to sleep. They guide the behaviours, beliefs and traditions of Aboriginal people. Sacred places, often marked by natural formations or cave paintings, are considered to be the footprints left by these spirits.

So, if you immerse yourself in these sacred stories, you will discover a priceless cultural richness, witness to an ancient civilization and deeply connected to the land.

Fact 25 - The boomerang is more than a toy

Perhaps, to you, the boomerang evokes a simple bent piece of wood that is thrown and returned. However, in Aboriginal culture, the boomerang holds a much deeper meaning and utility.

Historically, boomerangs were used as hunting weapons, musical instruments, or to dig into the earth. While some were indeed designed to return to their caster, others, because of their shape or weight, were intended for very specific tasks, such as hunting large animals.

Their manufacture requires great skill and in-depth knowledge of wood. Aboriginal people carefully choose the piece of wood, carve it with precision, and then often decorate it with symbolic motifs telling a story or rite.

So, the next time you see a boomerang or hold one in your hands, remember that it's not just a fun toy, but something deeply rooted in the history and culture of an ancient people.

Fact 26 - The Yolngu Artist Tribe

Do you know the Yolngu? This Aboriginal community in northern Australia is widely recognised for its rich artistic tradition. For thousands of years, they have been creating works that are not only beautiful but also tell the story of their people.

Their art is expressed in particular through bark paintings. Using natural pigments, the Yolngu illustrate scenes of daily life, mythological stories and maps of their lands. These works are often linked to the "Dream", a concept central to their cosmogony.

But their art doesn't stop there. They are also renowned for their ritual dances, chants and the making of the didgeridoo, Australia's emblematic instrument. The melodious and hypnotic sounds of the didgeridoo often accompany their ceremonies and tell ancestral stories.

As you delve into the art of the Yolngu, you discover not only their immense artistry, but also their deep connection to the land and how they preserve and pass on their culture through the generations.

Fact 27 - Aboriginal Festivals

Have you ever heard of Aboriginal festivals in Australia? These events are a vibrant explosion of culture, tradition and artistry, where the ancestral heritage of First Peoples is celebrated with pride and passion.

At these festivals, dance plays a central role. The dancers, dressed in traditional body paints, perform movements that tell stories from the "Dream", the complex mythology that shapes the Aboriginal worldview. As you watch them, you are transported to another world, a world of legends and connections with nature.

Singing, too, is fundamental. Accompanied by instruments such as the didgeridoo, the singers tell stories of love, land, sea and sky. Their voices resonate like an echo of ancient times, recalling the stories of their ancestors.

By participating in one of these festivals, you not only experience stunning performances, but also immerse yourself in the richness and depth of a culture that has survived and thrived for thousands of years.

Fact 28 - 250 Different Ancient Languages

Did you know that Australia is a real linguistic melting pot? Prior to European settlement, the continent was home to nearly 250 distinct Aboriginal languages, each with its own history, grammar and vocabulary.

Each language was deeply rooted in the land from which it came. For example, the words used in the language of the desert peoples were very different from those of the coastal communities. This linguistic diversity reflected how different groups interpreted and interacted with their environment.

Unfortunately, over time and due to a variety of factors, including colonization, many of these languages have become extinct or are in danger of extinction. Today, only about twenty of these languages are still spoken fluently.

However, there is hope. Many Aboriginal communities and dedicated linguists are working together to revitalise and preserve these linguistic treasures. By learning and understanding these languages, you connect to a rich and deep history that dates back thousands of years.

Fact 29 - Art of Stitches

Have you ever seen those beautiful paintings made up of thousands of little dots? This is stitch art, a traditional art technique of the Aboriginal peoples of Australia. These works are not only aesthetically pleasing, they also tell stories and represent maps of the territory.

Every stitch, every color and every pattern has a specific meaning. Artists use this technique to illustrate legends, dreams, and important events. For example, a circle could symbolize a waterhole or camp, while wavy lines could represent a stream.

However, not all the secrets of these paintings are revealed at first glance. Some details are reserved for insiders, for people who possess the knowledge to decipher these hidden messages.

So, the next time you come across one of these works of art, take a moment to stop and admire it. Behind every point lies a world rich in history, culture and spirituality.

Fact 30 - Ancestral Totems and Sculptures

Did you know that totem poles, these imposing wooden sculptures, are much more than just works of art? They reflect the culture and history of Australia's Aboriginal peoples. Each totem pole tells a story, symbolizes a legend, or represents an ancestor.

Carved directly from tree trunks, totem poles are often adorned with animals, human beings, and other shapes. Every detail, every motif has a meaning. A bird could symbolize a journey, while a snake could evoke transformation or rebirth.

But these sculptures are not only decorative. They play an essential role in Aboriginal ceremonies, marking important events, such as births or initiations. Totem poles are also seen as guardians, protecting the community and its territory.

The next time you look at a totem pole, remember that it is not just an artistic object, but a true testament to the cultural and historical richness of Australia's Aboriginal peoples.

Fact 31 - British Prisoners, Early Settlers

Australia, with its vast territories and wilderness, wasn't always as you know it today. Before the big cities came into being, this continent was mainly inhabited by Aboriginal peoples. But have you ever heard of how the British played a major role in the colonisation of Australia?

In the 18th century, Britain was looking for ways to dispose of its surplus of prisoners. The idea of sending them to Australia then emerged. In 1788, the "First Fleet", consisting of 11 ships, landed on the shores of what is now Sydney, with more than 700 prisoners on board.

These prisoners, often convicted of petty crimes, became the first European settlers on the continent. They had to adapt to a harsh environment, build shelters, cultivate the land and establish the first settlements.

This phase of Australia's history is complex, marked by conflicts with Indigenous peoples and the hardships of colonization. But it laid the foundation for the modern Australia we know today.

Fact 32 - ANZAC: War Hero

When you hear about ANZAC, do you really know what it refers to? ANZAC, or the Australian and New Zealand Army Corps, is much more than just a military alliance between Australia and New Zealand. It is a symbolic entity deeply rooted in the identity of these two nations.

The birth of ANZAC dates back to the First World War, during the Battle of Gallipoli in 1915. ANZAC troops, sent to support the Allies, found themselves facing fierce resistance from the Ottoman Empire. Despite the tragic outcome and heavy casualties, the bravery and camaraderie of these soldiers left a lasting impression.

Every year on April 25, Australia and New Zealand commemorate ANZAC Day to pay tribute to these heroes. This day has become a time of national remembrance, remembering the sacrifices of all soldiers.

So the next time you hear about ANZAC, you'll know it's more than just a piece of history. It is a legacy, a symbol of honour and pride for two nations.

Fact 33 - The Australian Gold Rush

Have you ever heard of the Great Gold Rush in Australia? In the mid-nineteenth century, this vast continent was the scene of one of the greatest gold fevers ever seen. This precious discovery literally transformed the Australian landscape and society.

It all started in 1851, when gold was discovered near Bathurst, New South Wales. Soon, news of similar discoveries emerged from other regions, attracting thousands of gold prospectors. These "diggings" or extraction zones became bustling cities almost overnight. People from all over the world, dreaming of wealth, flocked to Australia.

But it wasn't just a quest for riches. The gold rush also had profound social implications. It has fostered immigration, contributing to a multicultural Australian society. It also led to tensions, notably during the Eureka Rebellion of 1854, when miners revolted against the authorities.

The next time you see an Australian gold coin, think of those tumultuous times that shaped a nation, and all those who risked their lives in pursuit of a dazzling fortune.

Fact 34 - The Mining Revolution of the Eureka Riot

Did you know that the search for gold led to one of the largest revolts in Australian history? The Eureka Riot of 1854 was much more than just an altercation between miners and authorities. It was a real call for justice and democracy.

It all started in Ballarat, Victoria. The miners, frustrated by the expensive gold mining licenses and the brutal methods of the police, decided to speak out against the injustice. They built a barricade, the "Stockade Eureka", and pledged allegiance to the Southern Cross flag, a symbol of their resistance.

Unfortunately, their rebellion did not last long. Colonial forces attacked the stockade, causing the deaths of many miners. But their sacrifice was not in vain. The Eureka Riot sparked public awareness and major political changes.

Indeed, this revolt led to a reform of mineral rights and laid the foundations for a democratic system in Australia. Thus, beyond gold, Eureka has become a symbol of a nation that seeks justice and equality.

Fact 35 - Canberra: A Chosen Capital

Have you ever heard of a capital city created from scratch to resolve a rivalry? Canberra, the capital of Australia, has a rather unique origin. It is neither Sydney nor Melbourne, but it is the result of a compromise between these two giant cities.

At the end of the 19th century, Sydney and Melbourne vied for the title of national capital. Neither wanted to give way to the other. Faced with this impasse, the solution found was to build a brand new city halfway between them, specifically to be the capital.

The Canberra location was chosen for its strategic and climatic assets. In 1913, the foundation stone was laid, marking the official birth of this new city. Architect Walter Burley Griffin designed the city's plan, incorporating green spaces, artificial lakes, and radial avenues.

Today, Canberra is the political and administrative centre of Australia, home to Parliament and the official residence of the Governor General. More than just a city, it is a symbol of the unity and vision of the Australian nation.

Fact 36 - Edith Cowan, the first woman elected

Do you know who Edith Cowan is? This bold woman made Australian history by breaking gender barriers in politics. Her journey was one of determination and led her to become the first woman elected to an Australian parliament.

Born in 1861, Edith grew up in a difficult context after the tragic death of her mother. However, these hardships strengthened her commitment to social justice, education, and women's rights. In particular, she has worked for the well-being of underprivileged women and children.

In 1921, Edith achieved a monumental feat by being elected to the Western Australian Parliament. At that time, politics was an almost exclusively male field. His victory was therefore much more than just a seat in parliament; It was proof that women could actively and effectively participate in the governance of the country.

Today, Edith Cowan is celebrated as a trailblazer and inspiration. She paved the way for the many women who aspire to influence and shape the future of their country through politics.

Fact 37 - Australia in the Two World Wars

Australia, although far from the major theatres of combat in Europe, played a crucial role in both world wars. Do you know the extent to which the Australians became involved in these major conflicts?

During the First World War, Australia sent more than 400,000 men overseas, with tragic consequences: nearly 60,000 of them never returned. The Battle of Gallipoli in 1915 is particularly emblematic of the Australian involvement. Despite the military failure, it forged a national identity and a sense of camaraderie among Australians.

During the Second World War, Australia was directly threatened, notably by Japan. The famous Battle of Kokoda in New Guinea in 1942 is an example of the determination of Australian troops to protect their territory.

These two wars had a profound impact on the Australian nation. They reinforced its identity and commitment to peace, while reminding us of the high cost of conflict. Every year, ANZAC Day commemorates these events and pays tribute to the country's heroes.

Fact 38 - Surf's up! Beach & Culture

Ah, surfing! When you think of Australia, it's hard not to mention its iconic beaches and the surf culture that is closely linked to them. Do you realise how ingrained surfing is in the Australian way of life?

From the beginning of the 20th century, surfing took off on the Australian coasts. Beaches such as Bondi in Sydney or Bells Beach in Victoria have become must-see spots for wave lovers. These places are not only intended for the practice of sports, but they are also places to meet and share.

Surf culture has also influenced Australian music, fashion, and even cinema. Movies like "Bra Boys" or "Point Break" are the perfect example of this, capturing the spirit and energy of surfing.

Finally, whether it's for competition or just fun, surfing is much more than a sport in Australia. It's a passion, a philosophy and, for many, a way of life. So, are you ready to put on your wetsuit and ride the waves?

Fact 39 - Snowy Mountains

When you think of Australia, snow-capped mountains probably aren't the first thing that comes to mind. Yet, the Snowy Mountains are home to one of the most ambitious and impressive engineering projects in the country: the Snowy Mountains Hydro-Electric Scheme.

Initiated in the 1940s, this project aimed to divert water from rivers in the Snowy Mountains to inland rivers for irrigation. But that wasn't his only goal. It also aimed to generate hydroelectric power to meet Australia's growing energy needs.

The project lasted 25 years and required the collaboration of engineers and workers from all over the world. The result? Sixteen major dams, seven power plants and more than 140 km of tunnels through the mountains! A feat of engineering at the time.

Today, the Snowy Mountains Hydro-Electric Scheme remains a symbol of determination and innovation. If you have the opportunity to visit this region, you will certainly be amazed by the scale of this project and its importance to the country.

Fact 40 - Sydney 2000

The year 2000 marked a memorable chapter in Australia's history. Sydney, the country's iconic city, has put itself in the spotlight by hosting the Summer Olympics. During these games, the city shone, offering the whole world an unforgettable spectacle.

Sydney's purpose-built Olympic Park vibrated to the rhythm of athletic performances, broken records and palpable emotions. Who could forget the dazzling Olympic Stadium, or the magnificent water show at the Sydney Aquatic Centre? These facilities have not only hosted high-performance athletes, but they continue to serve the local community.

Cathy Freeman, an Australian Aboriginal athlete, has become an icon of these games. By lighting the Olympic flame and winning gold in the 400 metres, she symbolised the spirit of unity and national pride.

If you're heading to Sydney, don't hesitate to visit these historic sites. They will remind you of the time when the eyes of the world were on Australia, celebrating harmony, sportsmanship and extraordinary human achievements.

Fact 41 - The Frog Jockeys

Maybe you've been to a horse race, but have you ever heard of frog racing with jockeys? In Australia, these original races really exist and attract many curious and amused spectators.

Every year, in some parts of Australia, special events are held where little frogs are the stars of the track. But where it gets really weird is that these frogs carry "jockeys" on their backs, which are actually small weights or figurines, giving them the appearance of miniature jockeys in the middle of a race!

These races aren't just a source of entertainment; They are often organized for charitable causes or to support local community initiatives. Of course, the well-being of the frogs is a priority, and every effort is made to ensure their safety and comfort.

So, if you're in Australia at the right time, don't miss the opportunity to attend one of these races like no other! It's a once-in-a-lifetime experience that will give you a glimpse into Australians' sense of humour and originality.

Fact 42 - XXL rabbit fences

You may think that all fences are designed to demarcate a property or territory, but in Australia, a fence was built with a very specific objective: to prevent rabbits from invading agricultural land!

In the nineteenth century, rabbits introduced to Australia proliferated alarmingly, causing major damage to crops and native vegetation. To curb this threat, it was decided to build the longest rabbit fence in the world. And believe me, with a total length of more than 3,000 kilometres, it's a real feat of engineering!

While this fence has been effective in some areas, rabbits have unfortunately found ways to get past it in other areas. Despite everything, it remains an impressive testimony to human determination in the face of an environmental challenge.

If you're traveling to Australia, try to see this fence for yourself. It's a stark reminder of the impact of invasive species and the sometimes drastic measures humans take to protect their environment and resources.

Fact 43 - Cockroach Races

Maybe you've heard of horse racing or greyhound racing, but have you ever imagined cockroaches running towards the finish line? Well, in Australia, it's a reality and an event that attracts a lot of spectators!

Every year on Australia's National Day, hundreds of people gather in pubs and bars to watch these amazing races. The rules are simple: each participant brings their own cockroach, places it in the center of a circle, and waits to see which one will reach the edge first.

This tradition, while wacky, is a good example of Australian humour and their penchant for unique celebrations. Some participants even go so far as to give their cockroach a special name or paint it with bright colors to distinguish it from others.

So, if you're in Australia on January 26th, why not join the crowd? It's an experience you won't soon forget and will give you a fun glimpse into Australian popular culture!

Fact 44 - Thong Throwing

Do you know flip-flop toss? No, it's not a joke! In Australia, flip-flop throwing, or "Thong Throwing", is a competition that generates a lot of excitement and laughter. Who would have thought that one of the most iconic accessories on the beach would become the center of such an entertaining competition?

Every summer, at various events and festivals, Australians of all ages line up to see who can throw a flip-flop as far as possible. With a special technique and a strong arm, some participants can throw their flip-flops over impressive distances!

But it's not just a matter of distance. How the flip-flop lands matters too! There are rules about how the flip-flop should land, and points are awarded accordingly. It's a hilarious sight to behold, with flip-flops flying around.

So, next time you're in Australia during the summer season, join the fun! Who knows, you might even discover that you have a hidden talent for flip-flop toss!

Fact 45 - Sand Sculpting

Imagine walking on a beach and coming face to face with a life-size castle, mythical creatures, or even entire scenes from fairy tales, all carved out of the sand. In Australia, "Sand Sculpting" is not just a simple beach activity, it is a real art!

Every year, internationally renowned sand artists travel to Australia's beaches to compete in sand carving competitions. These masters of sand use special tools to carve detailed and stunning creations that attract thousands of spectators. These are not just small castles, but real ephemeral masterpieces!

One of the most famous events is the "Sand Sculpting Australia", where artists have specific themes to follow, pushing their creativity to the limit. The show is incredibly fascinating, showing that the beach can be a canvas for art.

Next time you're in Australia, don't forget to check out the sand carving events. You'll be amazed at what can be created with just sand and imagination!

Fact 46 - Bin Chicken, the Urban Bird

Do you know the iconic bird of Sydney's streets? No, it is not a colorful exotic species, but the "Bin Chicken", also known as the Sacred Ibis. Once considered sacred in Egypt, it has now adopted a very different lifestyle in Australia.

Originally, the Sacred Ibis lived in wetlands, feeding on small aquatic animals. But with increasing urbanization and the decrease in wetlands, this bird has adapted to a new environment: the city. Today, you can see him rummaging through garbage cans, looking for food scraps, hence his nickname "Bin Chicken".

This bird, with its long, curved beak and white feathers, has become a familiar and iconic figure in Australia's urban areas. It has even become a subject of humor and memes on social media.

If you're visiting Australia, keep an eye out for this strange urban resident. The Sacred Ibis is living proof of nature's ability to adapt to our ever-changing world.

Fact 47 - Big Things Everywhere

On your trip to Australia, you might be surprised by the many oversized structures that line roads and cities. These "Big Things" have become an integral part of Australia's tourism culture.

Since the 1960s, these structures, which can be animals, fruits, or even everyday objects, have been erected to attract tourists to small towns and rural areas. For example, in Coffs Harbour, you'll find a huge banana, and in Goulburn, you'll be greeted by a giant merino named "Big Merino".

But that's not all! Other famous structures include the "Big Pineapple" in Queensland and the "Big Lobster" in South Australia. These attractions have become so popular that there are now more than 150 of them in the entire country!

If you're heading to Australia, don't hesitate to take a detour to see some of these "Big Things". Not only are they fun to watch, but they also tell a story of Australia's unique history and culture.

Fact 48 - Cane Toad Race: A Slippery Competition

Have you ever heard of an unusual animal race in Australia? No, these are not horses or greyhounds, but buffalo toads, also called "Cane Toads" in English.

Introduced to Australia in the 1930s to control sugarcane field pests, these amphibians have rapidly multiplied, becoming a real scourge on the local ecosystem. But Australians, with their sense of humour and love for community events, have found a creative way to deal with this invader: organizing buffalo toad races!

In Queensland, at annual events like "Cane Toad Racing", these slippery creatures are placed in the centre of a circle, and the first to reach the periphery is crowned champion. Participants can bet on their favourite toad, and the funds raised are often donated to charity.

If you find yourself in the area at the time of these races, don't hesitate to stop by to witness this unusual spectacle. It's a quintessentially Australian experience, combining humour, camaraderie and a quirky approach to preserving the environment!

Fact 49 - Unusual Festivals

Australia is renowned for its unusual festivals, and among them, two stand out for their fruit celebration: the Mango Festival and the Melon Festival.

In Bowen, Queensland, the mango is king. Every year, this juicy and sweet fruit is celebrated at the "Bowen Mango Festival". Locals compete with each other with parades, mango sculptures and even competitions to devour this tropical fruit as quickly as possible. But that's not all: the event is also an opportunity to discover the importance of mango for the local economy.

On the other hand, in Chinchilla, also in Queensland, it is the melon that is in the spotlight. The "Melon Festival" offers activities that are original to say the least: cart races pulled by melons, melon tossing and even, for the more adventurous, melon skiing! Participants slide over large chunks of melon, creating bursts of laughter among the spectators.

If you have the opportunity to visit Australia during these festivities, don't miss these unique events. It's the perfect opportunity to immerse yourself in Australian culture, which is both quirky and warm.

Fact 50 - Anna Creek, the largest ranch in the world

Australia is a country of vast expanses, and among them is a particular gem: Anna Creek. Have you ever heard of this place? It's simply the largest ranch in the world, far surpassing anything you could imagine.

Located in South Australia, Anna Creek covers an impressive 23,677 square kilometres. To give you an idea, it's almost the size of Belgium! This huge territory is mainly dedicated to cattle breeding, with thousands of head of cattle roaming freely in the vast pastures.

With such a dimension, the challenges are numerous. How do you make sure the cattle are healthy or even just locate them? Ranch owners and caretakers use planes and helicopters to oversee the herds, exemplifying innovation in the service of tradition.

If you're traveling to Australia, a visit to Anna Creek will give you a unique perspective on large-scale farming and how passion and dedication can transform a wild landscape into a place of productivity.

Fact 51 - Aussie Rules

If you're looking for a sport that truly captures the Australian spirit and energy, look no further than "Aussie Rules". Officially known as Australian rules football, this game is a veritable institution here, fusing stamina, tactics and boundless passion.

The game originated in Australia in the 1850s, drawing inspiration in part from rugby and other ball sports. It is played on an oval court, with two teams of 18 players each. The goal? Score the most points by sending the ball between goal posts using your hands or feet. And believe me, the matches can get very intense!

One of the biggest competitions in this sport is the AFL (Australian Football League). Every year, teams from all over the country compete for the prestigious title. The AFL Grand Final, played in Melbourne, attracts thousands of spectators and is a major event in the Australian sporting calendar.

So, if you want to experience Australia in an authentic way, don't miss the opportunity to watch or, why not, play Aussie Rules. You will discover an essential part of our cultural identity!

Fact 52 - Sydney Opera House

Ah, the Sydney Opera House! As soon as you hear about Australia, this iconic structure probably comes to mind. Perched on Sydney Harbour, this building is much more than a performance venue, it is a national symbol.

Designed by Danish architect Jørn Utzon, the Sydney Opera House is an architectural feat with its intertwined white sail hulls. Inaugurated in 1973, this building was controversial during its design, but is now recognized as a marvel of the twentieth century. In fact, in 2007, UNESCO listed it as a World Heritage Site, highlighting its cultural and architectural significance.

Inside, the Opera House houses several rooms dedicated to the performing arts, hosting ballets, operas, plays and other shows. Attending a show here is an unforgettable experience, not only for the exceptional acoustics, but also for the spectacular setting.

If you're passing through Sydney, make a promise: take the time to visit the Opera House, day or night. It is an icon that deserves to be experienced up close, a testament to Australia's boldness and vision.

Fact 53 - Pavlova: sweet and delicious!

Ah, the pavlova! This meringue that's crispy on the outside and soft on the inside, topped with whipped cream and fresh fruit, is a delight you won't get tired of. If the name sounds familiar, it's because it's dedicated to the famous Russian ballerina Anna Pavlova.

The exact origin of this dessert is the subject of heated debate between Australia and New Zealand. Each country claims to be the creator, eager to take credit for this sweet wonder. What is certain is that this dessert was designed in honor of Anna Pavlova during her tour of the southern hemisphere in the 1920s.

Regardless of where it actually comes from, one thing is for sure: pavlova is now firmly entrenched in Australian food culture. On special occasions, parties and especially on hot summer days, it is often on the menu.

Next time you're craving sugar, think about pavlova. It's a delicacy that perfectly represents Australia's festive spirit and taste for good things.

Fact 54 - Vegemite: Love or Hate!

Ah, the Vegemite! This dark brown spread, salty and powerful in taste, is arguably one of Australia's most iconic foods. Made from brewer's yeast extract, it's rich in B vitamins and umami, that savory taste found in many fermented foods.

First introduced in 1923, Vegemite has become an integral part of Australian culture. It is not uncommon to see Australian children eating Vegemite sandwiches for breakfast or afternoon tea. However, for the uninitiated, its distinctive flavor can be a shock!

Opinions on Vegemite are clear. Some love it, considering it a comfort and nutritious food, while others find it simply inedible. But it's precisely this divide that makes it such a popular topic of conversation.

If you've never tried Vegemite, go for it! You might be pleasantly surprised or join the ranks of those who frown. Either way, it's a decidedly Australian taste experience not to be missed.

Fact 55 - Meat Pies: The Favorite Snack

Discover meat pies, these small pies filled with meat that have been the delight of Australians for generations. Both simple and delicious, they embody the gourmet spirit of Australia. Typically made with crispy puff pastry filled with ground beef, onions, and gravy, these pies are a bite of comfort.

Historically, meat pies have their origins in Europe, but Australia has adopted and adapted them to make them a national icon. You can find them almost everywhere, from football stadiums to small local bakeries. They are often accompanied by "tomato sauce", an Australian version of ketchup.

At sporting events, it's not uncommon to see fans enthusiastically biting into a meat pie while supporting their favorite team. It's a tradition that brings Australians of all ages and backgrounds together.

So, if you're in Australia, don't miss the opportunity to enjoy a meat pie. It's more than just a snack, it's a cultural experience to be savoured to the fullest!

Fact 56 - Akubra, the Australian hat

The Akubra is not just a hat: it is a symbol of Australian identity. Instantly recognizable, it stands out for its wide brim and rugged design, designed to withstand the harshest conditions of the Australian bush. Made from high-quality rabbit felt, the Akubra protects against the scorching sun and sudden rains.

Since its inception in the early 20th century, the Akubra has become an indispensable companion for rural workers, herders, and even some city dwellers. It is not uncommon to see personalities, such as prime ministers or movie stars, wearing an Akubra, thus affirming their Australian pride.

But beyond its practical function, the Akubra has sentimental value. For many, it evokes memories of outdoor adventures, days spent on horseback, or shared moments around a campfire under the stars.

So, if you're visiting Australia, why not adopt this national emblem? It could well become your best ally against the vagaries of the Australian weather!

Fact 57 - Thongs: not what you think!

Ah, the "thongs"! If you hear this word and immediately think of a type of underwear, think again. In Australia, the term "thongs" actually refers to flip-flops, those lightweight shoes that are easy to put on and are perfect for a day at the beach.

Historically, flip flops originated in Asia and have been adopted by many cultures around the world. But in Australia, they have become an integral part of clothing culture. Whether it's hot or cool, you'll always find someone with thongs on their feet, taking a leisurely stroll along the coast or barbecuing in the backyard.

And if you go to Australia, you'll quickly notice how popular they are. In some coastal areas, it's not uncommon to see signs saying "No Shirt, No Shoes, No Service" turned into "No Shirt, No Thongs, No Service"!

So, the next time you hear about "thongs" in Australia, you'll know exactly what they are. And why not, you could even buy a pair as a souvenir!

Fact 58 - G'day mate

When you think of Australia, chances are the phrase "G'day mate" comes to mind. And for good reason, it's one of the country's most iconic greetings. "G'day" is actually a contraction of "Good Day", and "mate" is a term of endearment for a friend.

Used for generations, this informal greeting is representative of the casual and friendly nature of Australians. Whether on the busy streets of Sydney or in the remote hinterland, you will be greeted with a warm "G'day mate" that will make you feel at home.

However, context is key. Although widely accepted, this expression is mostly used among friends or in informal situations. If you're going to a business meeting or formal event, it's best to stick to a simple "Good morning" or "Good afternoon".

So, if one day you find yourself in Australia, don't hesitate to greet the locals with a happy "G'day mate"! You'll be surprised how much this little phrase opens doors and smiles.

Fact 59 - Australia Day: BBQ & Celebrations

Every year on January 26th, Australia celebrates. It's Australia Day. This date commemorates the arrival of the first British fleet in Sydney in 1788. For many, it's a day of national celebration, marked by fireworks, concerts, and, of course, outdoor barbecues!

Barbecuing is indeed a tradition deeply rooted in Australian culture. During Australia Day, parks and beaches fill up with families and friends gathering to grill sausages, steaks and prawns. While listening to music and sipping a cold drink, the sense of community is palpable.

But this day is not without controversy. For the Aboriginal peoples of Australia, this date is a reminder of the European invasion and the loss of their lands. That's why some call it "Invasion Day" and are campaigning for a date change.

Regardless, Australia Day remains an iconic day, where the entire country pauses to celebrate, reflect and come together in a spirit of unity and diversity.

Fact 60 - Triple J Hottest 100

Ah, the Triple J Hottest 100! If you're an Australian music lover, you're bound to know this phenomenon. Every year at the end of January, Australia's national radio station Triple J compiles a list of the top 100 songs from the previous year, based on listeners' votes. It's a must-see musical event in Australia.

Since its launch in 1989, this list has grown in popularity and has become a veritable institution. Listeners actively participate by voting for their favorite tracks. The countdown is broadcast on the national holiday, Australia Day, creating a perfect soundtrack for the celebrations.

Artists from all over the world aspire to be present in this prestigious list, as being ranked in the Hottest 100 is considered a true honor. Bands such as Arctic Monkeys, Tame Impala, and Billie Eilish have all been crowned number one over the years.

For many Australians, the Triple J Hottest 100 is more than just a playlist: it's a tradition, a moment of sharing and musical discovery, a reflection of the trends and tastes of the moment.

Fact 61 - Sunbathing

When you think of Australia, you probably picture golden beaches bathed in sunlight. Indeed, Australia is often associated with an outdoor lifestyle, with a particular penchant for sunbathing. With its endless stretches of coastline and enviable climate, it's the perfect place to lie down and sunbathe.

However, sunbathing is not just a simple recreational activity here. It is an integral part of Australian culture. On weekends and holidays, the beaches fill up with locals and tourists looking to soak up the country's bountiful sunshine. Bondi Beach in Sydney or Surfers Paradise on the Gold Coast are perfect examples.

But be careful! Australia is also very proactive in raising awareness of the dangers of the sun. Campaigns like "Slip, Slop, Slap" encourage everyone to cover up, put on sunscreen, and wear a hat. Sun protection is essential in a country where the sun can be so unforgiving.

So, if you're planning to enjoy the Australian sun, always remember to take precautions. Embrace the lifestyle in the sun, but do it responsibly!

Fact 62 - Black Box

Have you ever heard of the "black box" in the context of aviation? This crucial invention is actually bright orange, and it was created by an Australian, Dr. David Warren. Thanks to him, the aviation industry has made huge strides in safety.

The black box, or flight recorder, is a device that records conversations in the cockpit as well as the aircraft's flight data. In the event of an accident, it provides valuable information that can help determine the cause. The idea came to David Warren in the 1950s, after a series of unsolved accidents.

In 1958, his prototype, called "Flight Memory", was introduced. Although it initially met with some resistance, the effectiveness of the device soon became apparent. Today, black boxes are mandatory on commercial aircraft around the world.

So, every time you board a plane, think of this Australian invention that has gone a long way in making air travel safer for all of us!

Fact 63 - Wi-Fi: technology made in Australia

Can you imagine a world without Wi-Fi? That would be difficult, wouldn't it? And did you know that this ubiquitous technology has its roots in Australia? Yes, that's right! The invention of Wi-Fi was largely the result of the efforts of Australian scientists.

It all started with the Commonwealth Scientific and Industrial Research Organisation (CSIRO) in Australia. In the 1990s, a team led by Dr. John O'Sullivan developed a key technology that would become a fundamental part of modern Wi-Fi. They initially sought to detect mini black holes, but their research eventually led them to revolutionize the way we connect to the internet.

Their discoveries resulted in a patent in 1996, which laid the foundation for Wi-Fi technology. Today, every time you connect wirelessly, whether it's with your smartphone, tablet or computer, it's thanks to this Australian invention.

So, next time you're surfing the net at your favorite coffee shop, think about these Australian scientists who made it all possible!

Fact 64 - Sunscreen Spray

Did you know that one of the most important advances in protecting your skin from the scorching sun comes from Australia? This is indeed the case, the anti-sun spray, a crucial invention for those who live under sunny skies, is an Australian pride.

Australia, known for its stretches of beaches and sunny days, is also unfortunately known for having one of the highest rates of skin cancer in the world. This has led researchers to look for effective ways to protect the skin. In the 1960s, Australian pharmacist Milton Blake began working on a lotion to protect the skin, which later became the sunscreen spray we know today.

This easy-to-apply spray offered effective protection against the sun's harmful rays, and therefore gained popularity not only in Australia but around the world. Next time you're getting ready for a day at the beach, spraying on this life-saving spray, remember the Australian ingenuity behind that bottle!

Fact 65 - Esky: Keep Everything Cool

Ah, the Esky! If you've never heard this term, let me introduce it to you. It's one of Australia's most beloved inventions, especially on hot summer days. The Esky, in other words, is a portable cooler, but for many Australians, it's much more than that.

Born in Australia in the 1950s, the Esky was designed to keep drinks and food cold for long periods of time, especially when traveling or picnics. With Australia's warm and sunny climate, it's easy to see why this invention has become so popular and indispensable.

Beyond its obvious usefulness, the Esky has become a cultural symbol. Think of those convivial moments with friends, around a barbecue, where everyone brings back their Esky filled with cold drinks and delicacies to share. It's a must-have part of outdoor gatherings.

So, if one day you find yourself in Australia, looking for a way to keep your cold beer or sandwich away from the heat, don't forget to thank the inventive spirit of this country and invest in a good old Esky!

Fact 66 - Cochlear Implant

Have you ever heard of the cochlear implant? This little technological marvel, which originated in Australia, has literally changed the lives of thousands of people with profound deafness. It's an invention that restores hearing!

The cochlear implant, developed in the 1970s by Dr. Graeme Clark in Melbourne, is an electronic device that helps people with hearing loss perceive sound. Unlike traditional hearing aids, which simply amplify sound, the cochlear implant bypasses damaged parts of the inner ear to directly stimulate the auditory nerve.

This was a revolutionary breakthrough. Imagine for a moment: children born deaf hearing their parents' voices for the first time, or adults rediscovering sounds they thought were lost forever. The emotional impact is immense.

If you ever come across someone with a small device behind their ear, know that this little gem of technology, born in Australia, may allow them to hear the world around them. A real feat that deserves to be saluted!

Fact 67 - Pacemaker

Do you know that little medical device that discreetly beats in the chest of many people? This is the pacemaker, an incredible invention that regulates the heartbeat of those whose hearts do not beat regularly on their own. And imagine that the first concepts of this lifesaver were developed in Australia!

Dr. Mark Lidwill, a Sydney anaesthetist, in collaboration with engineer Edgar Booth, created the first pacemaker in 1926. Although rudimentary, this device was the precursor to modern versions, using electrical impulses to stimulate the heart and maintain a steady rhythm.

Today, these devices are tiny, highly sophisticated, and can be implanted directly into the body. They have literally changed and saved thousands of lives. People with cardiac arrhythmias, who previously would have had a reduced quality of life, can now live normal lives thanks to this technology.

So the next time you hear about the pacemaker, remember this Australian story and the pioneers who paved the way for this medical revolution!

Fact 68 - Plastic Money

When you open your wallet, have you ever noticed those bills that seem more durable than traditional paper? Maybe you even found them a little slippery to the touch? These banknotes are actually made from a special form of plastic, and this innovation came straight from Australia!

In 1988, Australia introduced the world's first polymer banknote, with the main objective of combating counterfeiting. These banknotes are not only harder to imitate, but they also have the advantage of being water-resistant, less likely to tear, and more durable than their paper counterparts.

Since that invention, more than 25 other countries have adopted the polymer banknote, recognizing its benefits in terms of safety and longevity. If you're traveling, you might even come across these tickets in countries like Canada, the United Kingdom, or Singapore.

Next time you hold one of these notes in your hand, think of this amazing Australian innovation that has transformed the way money is printed around the world!

Fact 69 - Google Maps: An Australian Involved!

Did you know that every time you use Google Maps, you're indirectly in contact with a brilliant Australian contribution? Yes, behind this must-have navigation tool is a creative Australian spirit.

Lars and Jens Eilstrup Rasmussen, two brothers, developed a start-up named "Where 2 Technologies" in 2003. Although Lars is of Danish descent, it was in Sydney that he settled and where this innovation was born. Their idea was to create a web-based mapping application rather than traditional software to download.

Google quickly spotted the potential of their invention and acquired "Where 2 Technologies" in 2004. Transforming and integrating this technology, Google Maps was launched in 2005. Today, who could imagine travelling without consulting this service?

Next time you're looking for directions or exploring a new city with Google Maps, remember the key role an Australian played in making it possible!

Fact 70 - The Black Box Rotation

When you think of the "black box" of airplanes, have you ever considered that it could also play a crucial role in rescue at sea? This is precisely what the black box rotation, an ingenious Australian innovation, does.

The idea was born out of the need to quickly locate ships in distress. Just like the black box on airplanes, this technology records vital data. But it has a peculiarity: in the event of a problem, it detaches and floats on the surface, emitting distress signals to facilitate the location of the ship.

This ingenious device was implemented in the aftermath of maritime tragedies where rescue efforts took a long time to locate the damaged ships. Thanks to the rotation of the black box, the response time was significantly reduced, increasing the chances of rescue.

The next time you hear about a successful rescue at sea, don't forget the contribution of this Australian technology that probably played a decisive role!

Fact 71 - Barrier Reef: World Wonder

Have you ever dreamed of diving into a vibrant underwater world? The Great Barrier Reef, located in Australia, is the perfect place for this. It is not only the largest coral reef system in the world, but also one of the most impressive natural wonders on the planet.

Stretching over 2,300 kilometres along the Queensland coast, it is home to incredible biodiversity. Thousands of species, from multicolored fish to majestic turtles, have made it their home. Every year, divers from all over the world come to admire this marine splendor.

But this treasure is under threat. Climate change, pollution and other factors are taking a toll on this fragile ecosystem. Considerable efforts are being made to protect and preserve the barrier reef for future generations.

So, if you have the chance to visit this wonder, do so with respect and admiration. It is a world heritage that we must cherish and preserve.

Fact 72 - Dugongs: Majestic Creatures

Have you ever heard of dugongs? These marine mammals, often referred to as "sea cows," are one of a kind. With their tapered bodies and wing-like pectoral fins, dugongs are the only strict marine herbivores, feeding primarily on seagrass.

Native to the warm waters of Australia, particularly the Great Barrier Reef, these elegant creatures are graceful swimmers. Despite their large size, they move with astonishing ease, gliding smoothly through the water, captivating anyone lucky enough to observe them.

But, like so many other marine species, dugongs are endangered. Habitat loss, pollution and collisions with boats are all hazards that weigh on them. Efforts are underway to protect these animals and their unique environment.

So, if you ever find yourself near Australian waters, keep an eye out. You might be lucky enough to catch a glimpse of one of these majestic creatures, a symbol of the beauty and fragility of marine life.

Fact 73 - Australian Sharks

Ah, sharks! These deep-sea predators often evoke fear in many people. Did you know that Australian waters are home to a wide variety of sharks, from towering great whites to harmless nurse sharks?

Australia's beaches are renowned for their perfect waves and golden sand, but they are also known for their underwater inhabitants. When swimming, it's good to know that safety measures are in place. Shark nets and aerial surveillance programs are often used to protect swimmers and surfers.

However, it is essential to understand that shark attacks remain extremely rare. Sharks don't usually try to prey on humans. Incidents are often the result of misunderstandings or confusion.

So the next time you're on an Australian beach, remember to respect these awe-inspiring creatures. After all, it's their natural habitat. With caution and respect, we can coexist with these kings of the oceans.

Fact 74 - Turtles: Birth at Mon Repos!

Mon Repos, in Australia, is not only a beautiful place; It is also a vital sanctuary for sea turtles. Have you ever dreamed of seeing the miracle of a turtle's birth up close? Mon Repos offers you this unique opportunity.

Every year, between November and March, green turtles and loggerheads, among others, climb the beach of Mon Repos to lay their eggs in the sand. This nocturnal show is a delicate dance, where the mother carefully digs a nest before depositing her precious loads.

About eight weeks later, these eggs hatch, and hundreds of little turtles make their first frantic run to the ocean, guided by the light of the moon. This moment is both touching and vulnerable, as many predators lie in wait for these little creatures.

If you go to My Rest during this time, you will witness one of nature's greatest miracles. However, don't forget that tranquility and caution are essential so as not to disturb these crucial moments in the turtles' lives.

Fact 75 - Box Jellyfish: Tiny but Mighty!

You've probably heard of the jellyfish, but do you know the box jellyfish? Native to Australian waters, this aquatic creature is small, but don't let its size fool you. It is one of the most venomous creatures on the planet.

Transparent and almost invisible in the water, the Box jellyfish can be up to 20 centimetres wide, with tentacles that can stretch up to three metres. A simple touch can be extremely painful for humans and, in some cases, even fatal.

If you decide to swim in Australian waters, exercise caution, especially during jellyfish season which usually runs from November to May. Many beaches in the north of the country install protective nets and offer vinegar, a remedy commonly used to treat jellyfish stings.

So, if you find yourself in front of this dangerous beauty, keep your distance! And don't forget, the sea is their territory; We are simply visitors. Respect these creatures and their habitat, and you'll be able to enjoy all the wonders the ocean has to offer.

Fact 76 - Nudibranchs: marine beauties!

Do you know about nudibranchs? These small, shellless marine molluscs are true jewels of the oceans. Renowned for their bright colors and stunning shapes, nudibranchs are often referred to as the "butterflies of the sea."

There are more than 3,000 species of nudibranchs, each with its own unique design and color palette. While diving, you might be lucky to come across electric blue specimens, bright oranges, or even patterns that look like an abstract work of art. These patterns aren't just aesthetic; They often warn predators of their toxicity.

Nudibranchs are fascinating creatures to study. For example, some feed on corals or anemones and can store toxins or stinging cells from their prey to defend themselves against predators.

Next time you're diving in Australian waters or other tropical seas, keep an eye out for these wonders. Respect their space and admire these natural masterpieces from afar. Who knows? You might be amazed by the hidden beauty of the underwater world!

Fact 77 - The Unique Fish of Lord Howe Island

Lord Howe Island, located between Australia and New Zealand, is a real treasure trove for marine wildlife enthusiasts. A UNESCO World Heritage Site, this island is home to an incredibly diverse marine ecosystem.

As you dive into the crystal clear waters surrounding the island, you'll discover a myriad of brightly colored and oddly shaped fish. The endemicity is remarkable: nearly 15% of the reef fish are unique to this region. That's an impressive rate when you consider that tropical waters are already teeming with thousands of species!

An iconic example is Lord Howe's sawfish, which can't be found anywhere else on the planet. This fish, with its prehistoric allure and distinctive shape, is a living reminder of the island's evolutionary history.

If you have the opportunity to visit Lord Howe's Island, don't forget your mask and snorkel. Each dive will introduce you to creatures you'll probably never see anywhere else. It's a journey through time, to encounter nature in its purest form.

Fact 78 - Dolphins at Monkey Mia

Monkey Mia, located on the west coast of Australia, has become famous for an absolutely magical natural spectacle. Every morning, at the edge of its crystal clear waters, a pod of wild dolphins approaches the shore, providing visitors with an unforgettable experience.

These curious and friendly dolphins have formed a special relationship with humans over the years. They approach spontaneously, without any prompting, creating incredible moments of interaction. If you look closely, you will be able to recognize some individuals by their distinctive marks and scars, as many of them are regular visitors.

It's one of the few places in the world where you can experience such closeness with these marine mammals in their natural habitat. Of course, it is essential to follow the guidelines given by the park rangers to ensure the safety and well-being of the dolphins.

So, if you're traveling to Australia, don't miss the opportunity to visit Monkey Mia. This is more than just an observation; It is a communion with nature that remains forever engraved in the memory.

Fact 79 - Mimetic Octopuses: Perfect Camouflage!

In Australia's waters, we find a sea creature with fascinating intelligence: the mimetic octopus. Unlike other octopuses that simply change color to blend in with their surroundings, this one goes further. It mimics not only the colors, but also the shapes and behaviors of other marine animals.

Imagine watching a lionfish for a moment and in the blink of an eye, it turns into an octopus! This is exactly what the mimetic octopus does. For example, it can take on the appearance of a flatfish, a stingray, or even a venomous sea snake, all to escape its predators or hunt discreetly.

This remarkable talent is the result of an evolution over millions of years. This ability to mimic several different animals clearly distinguishes it from other octopus species. Nature, in its wisdom, has provided him with an unparalleled survival tool.

Next time you dive near the Australian coast, watch carefully! You could be admiring a mimetic octopus without even realizing it.

Fact 80 - The Dance of the Manta Rays

When you dive into Australian waters, you might witness an unforgettable sight: the graceful dance of manta rays. With a wingspan of up to seven metres, these giants of the seas glide with unparalleled grace, performing movements reminiscent of those of prima ballerina.

It is not only their grace that fascinates, but also their intelligence. Did you know that manta rays have one of the largest brains of any fish? This makes them particularly curious, and it is not uncommon for them to approach divers to observe them, creating memorable encounters.

But manta rays aren't just curious. They play a vital role in the marine ecosystem. Feeding mainly on plankton, they help regulate the population of these tiny organisms, thus ensuring a balance in the food chain.

If you're lucky enough to see them in action, take a moment to admire these majestic ocean dancers. Their beauty and elegance are a true gift from nature.

Fact 81 - Bunyip: The Billabong Monster!

Have you ever heard of the Bunyip? It is a mythical creature that, according to Aboriginal legends, inhabits billabongs, freshwater ponds formed by the ancient meanders of rivers in Australia. The Bunyip is one of the most enigmatic figures in Australian mythology, and his descriptions vary greatly between regions and histories.

Some say it looks like a huge emu with long claws, while others describe it as an aquatic beast with fangs and a mane. Despite these differences, one thing remains constant: the frightening cry of the Bunyip. This call, often compared to that of an animal in distress, would be a warning to anyone who gets too close to their territory.

If you're walking by a billabong on a dark night, you might wonder if the Bunyip is real or just a figment of the ancients' imagination. But one thing is for sure, this legend has become deeply ingrained in Australian culture, reminding us of the importance of the stories that shape a nation's identity.

So, the next time you hear a mysterious scream near a billabong, beware! The Bunyip may well be on the prowl.

Fact 82 - Ned Kelly: Legendary Outlaw!

Do you know Ned Kelly, that name that resonates in Australian history? Born in 1854, this son of Irish immigrants became one of Australia's most notorious outlaws. His story is that of a rebel, a bandit, and a folk hero all at once, depending on one's point of view.

From a young age, Kelly was embroiled in run-ins with the police. But it was in 1878, after the alleged attempted murder of a policeman, that Ned and his gang became Australia's most wanted fugitives. Over the course of two years, they committed numerous robberies and repeatedly evaded capture, reinforcing their status as legends.

One of Ned Kelly's most iconic images is of his homemade armor, designed to protect him from bullets during his final confrontation with the police at Glenrowan in 1880. Unfortunately for him, this armor wasn't enough to save him.

Today, Ned Kelly is seen by some as a symbol of resistance to British oppression, while others see him simply as a criminal. In any case, his legend lives on and fascinates as ever.

Fact 83 - Tiddalik: Frog of Legend!

Have you ever wondered where the myths and legends that shape a nation's culture come from? Australia is full of these stories, and one of the most famous is that of Tiddalik, the frog. This Aboriginal legend tells a tale about the origin of the waters in Australia.

According to legend, Tiddalik woke up one day with an insatiable thirst. He began to drink all the water he could find, from rivers, lakes, to small ponds. Very quickly, the Australian continent became dry, causing distress to many creatures who depended on these water sources for their livelihoods.

In the face of this disaster, the animals came together to find a solution. They decided to make Tiddalik laugh to force him to spit out all the water he had absorbed. After several attempts, it was the snake Nabunum who, with his contortions, managed to make the frog laugh, thus returning the water to the earth.

This story, told from generation to generation, serves as a reminder of the importance of balance in nature and the need to respect the resources our Earth offers us.

Fact 84 - Yowie: Bigfoot from Australia!

Have you ever heard of Bigfoot or Sasquatch? These legendary creatures are well known in North America. But did you know that Australia has its own Bigfoot? Yes, you heard that right! Australians call it "Yowie", a creature shrouded in mystery and folklore.

The earliest mentions of the Yowie date back to Aboriginal accounts. These beings, described as bipedal, hairy, and large, lived in the mountains and dense forests of Australia. Aborigines often portrayed them as timid but powerful beings, who avoided contact with humans.

Over the centuries, many Australians have claimed to have seen the Yowie. Mysterious footprints, sightings and even a few blurry photos continue to fuel the debate about its existence. This evidence is often controversial, but it stirs up curiosity and excitement about this legend.

Today, the Yowie has become an icon of Australian popular culture. While its biological reality remains a matter of debate, its impact on the country's narratives and imagination is undeniable.

Fact 85 - Quinkan, the spirit of the rocks!

When you think of Australia, your mind may wander to its beaches, unique wildlife, or desert landscapes. But are you aware of its equally fascinating Aboriginal legends? The Quinkans, ancestral spirits carved in stone, are one of these legends.

According to Aboriginal accounts, the Quinkan are rock spirits who inhabit the Laura Plateau in Far North Queensland. These spirits, which can be benevolent or mischievous, have the ability to appear and disappear at will in rock formations. Their depictions, visible in the form of cave paintings, are an eloquent testimony to the rich Aboriginal culture.

These paintings, often done in ochre, show slender figures, sometimes with disproportionate legs and arms. They tell stories of interactions between humans and these spirits, life lessons, ceremonies and rituals. Painting sites are considered sacred and are often off the beaten path.

If you're visiting Australia, make an effort to explore these remote areas and immerse yourself in these ancient legends. As you look at these paintings, you may feel the presence of the Quinkans, who have been watching over their land since time immemorial.

Fact 86 - The Black Dog, the Disturbing Spirit!

If you like stories that give you goosebumps, you may have heard of the legend of the black dog. Far from being a mere folkloric creature, this canine ghost is a disturbing figure that haunts the legends of many cultures, especially in Britain.

These ghost dogs, often described as large, black canines with bright eyes, often appear at night, especially on roads, swamps, and near intersections. Some say they are the guardians of the portals leading to the afterlife, while others believe they portend death. Stories abound of frightening encounters with these beasts, fading as quickly as they appeared.

A famous example is the Black Shuck of East Anglia, England. In 1577, according to the chronicles, a black dog broke into Blythburgh Church, killing two people and leaving claw marks still visible today.

So, next time you're out for a walk at night, be careful! Who knows if the black dog isn't lurking in the shadows, ready to cross your path?

Fact 87 - Rainbow Serpent, the creator of the world!

Have you ever heard of the Rainbow Serpent? This sacred entity, known as the "Rainbow Serpent", occupies a central place in the mythologies and beliefs of the Aboriginal peoples of Australia.

The Rainbow Snake is seen as a powerful and benevolent being, often associated with water, rain, lakes and rivers. It is he who, according to legends, shaped the mountains, valleys and waterways of the Australian continent as he moved across the country. These movements created the distinctive features of the Australian landscape.

Numerous stories and cave paintings depict this impressive being. For example, in Kakadu National Park in Northern Australia, cave paintings depict the Rainbow Serpent and tell stories related to its presence.

The next time you're admiring a rainbow or strolling by a waterway in Australia, remember the mighty Rainbow Serpent and its vital role in the creation of the Aboriginal world.

Fact 88 - Drop Bears: Myth or Reality?

Ah, the "Drop Bears"! These creatures often evoke curiosity, awe, and laughter in those who visit Australia. But what are they really?

"Drop Bears" are described as large, carnivorous koalas-like animals that fall from trees to attack their prey, usually unsuspecting humans. These creatures have a reputation for being aggressive and dangerous, especially to tourists.

But rest assured, the "Drop Bears" are just an Australian urban legend, a joke that locals like to tell visitors. This myth is often used to tease and amuse travellers, playing on the world's fascination with Australia's unique wildlife.

So the next time you're out in Australia and someone warns you about the "Drop Bears", you'll know it's a local joke. But that doesn't make the story any less fun or memorable, does it?

Fact 89 - Wandjinas, the Spirit of Rain!

Have you ever heard of the Wandjinas? These iconic figures are at the heart of the beliefs of the indigenous peoples of the Kimberley, in north-west Australia.

The Wandjinas are considered to be ancestral spirits of rain and clouds. They are often depicted in rock art with large faces without mouths, eyes set apart and surrounded by stripes or halos, symbolizing lightning and rain. These mystical images have been painted on rock faces for millennia and continue to be re-painted today, evidence of their enduring importance to Indigenous cultures.

According to tradition, it is thanks to the Wandjinas that the rain falls and the rivers flow. They have the ability to cause storms and are respected as creators and protectors. The laws and customs that govern the representation of the Wandjinas are strict, reflecting their sacred status.

Next time you visit Australia, look for these impressive images. They offer a unique window into a rich and ancient culture that deeply reveres the forces of nature.

Fact 90 - Sky Heroes, Aboriginal Stars!

You've probably seen the starry sky before, but did you know that the Aboriginal people of Australia see their own heroes and stories there? The night sky is much more than just a sight for them.

Constellations, for Indigenous peoples, are not just groupings of stars. They tell stories, pass on life lessons and ancestral laws. For example, the famous constellation of Orion, which you might know as the "Hunter", is interpreted by some Aboriginal groups as a hunter's club surrounded by three women represented by the "three sisters" (Orion's three bright stars).

The Milky Way also has its own meanings. They can represent rivers of fish, snakes, or other mythical creatures and heroes. These stories vary from region to region, reflecting the richness and diversity of Aboriginal cultures.

The next time you look up at the night sky, remember that it's filled with stories and traditions that date back millennia. Heaven, for Aboriginal people, is an open book filled with eternal tales.

Fact 91 - Australia: beaches as far as the eye can see!

When we think of Australia, how can we not think of its legendary beaches? With more than 50,000 km of coastline, Australia offers you a multitude of sandy horizons, among the most beautiful in the world.

Bondi Beach in Sydney, for example, is arguably one of the most famous beaches. Popular with surfers and swimmers, it is the symbol of Australia's seaside culture. However, beyond the urban beaches, there are countless wilderness areas where nature reigns supreme, such as Whitehaven Beach with its incredibly white sand.

But Australia doesn't stop at its tourist beaches. Some of its coastlines are still unknown and offer an authentic experience. There, away from the crowds, you can feel the vastness of the continent and the power of the ocean.

The next time you're dreaming of escapism, think of Australia and its endless beaches. Whether you're looking for a surfing adventure, a leisurely swim or a moment of solitude by the sea, Australia is bound to have a beach for you.

Fact 92 - "She'll be right": casual attitude

If you travel to Australia, you'll surely hear the expression "She'll be right". More than just a phrase, it's a mantra that reflects Australians' laid-back and optimistic attitude to life.

This saying, which can be translated as "it will be fine" or "everything will be fine", shows how Australians approach situations with a certain serenity. For example, if you misplace your car keys at a barbecue with friends, instead of panicking, a local might pat you on the shoulder and tell you "She'll be right," encouraging you to stay calm and look on the bright side.

But be careful! This does not mean that Australians take everything lightly. They recognize the importance of working hard and facing challenges. It's simply their way of reminding us that sometimes you have to let go, accept the ups and downs and believe that everything will work out in the end.

So, the next time you find yourself in a stressful situation, why not adopt the "She'll be right" attitude? You'll see, it can really help to see things in a more positive light!

Fact 93 - Giant Sand Dunes: Adventures in Lancelin!

Have you ever imagined standing atop a sand dune, gazing out over an almost endless expanse of sandy hills? Lancelin, Western Australia, offers this unique experience. Its giant sand dunes are a major attraction for adventurers from all over the world.

These dunes, among the largest in the southern hemisphere, offer a multitude of activities. Many come for sandboarding, gliding enthusiastically down the slopes. If you're looking for something a little more motorized, quad biking is also popular, letting enthusiasts venture out at high speeds over these changing terrains.

But that's not all! Apart from adventure, the dunes offer breathtaking panoramas, especially at sunset. When the last light of day illuminates the sand, it's as if the desert is ablaze, offering hues of pink, orange and purple.

If you find yourself in Western Australia, don't miss the opportunity to visit Lancelin. It's the perfect place to combine thrills and natural beauty, creating memories that will last a lifetime.

Fact 94 - Some Spiders Are Nice

Australia is often associated with dangerous spiders, isn't it? But did you know that the vast majority of Australian spiders are completely harmless to humans? Yes, that's right, and some are even beneficial to the environment and humans.

Take, for example, the gold-weaver spider. It is famous for its sparkling golden canvas that glistens in the sun. Not only is it beautiful to watch, but it also catches a wide variety of insect pests. It is a natural ally to maintain balance in our gardens.

And then there's the jumping spider. These little creatures are not only harmless, but they are also curious and playful. They tend to jump from one place to another, hence their name, and are fascinating to observe up close.

Finally, keep in mind that even venomous spiders, such as the dreaded funnel-web spider, usually prefer to avoid humans. So, the next time you come across a spider in Australia, remember that not all spiders are to be feared. Some can even be considered friends!

Fact 95 - The Lyrebird's Wing Beats

You may have heard of the lyrebird, this Australian bird with a beautiful tail and resemblance to a lyre. But what's really fascinating about this bird isn't just its appearance, but its ability to mimic a multitude of sounds with astonishing accuracy!

If you're walking in the forest and suddenly you hear the sound of a chainsaw, don't be alarmed right away. It could just be a lyrebird nearby! These birds can mimic the sound of machines, other animals, and even human voices. All this with an accuracy that will leave you speechless.

Their repertoire is not limited to a few sounds. Some lyrebirds are known to mimic more than twenty different bird species in a single singing session. Imagine a bird reproducing the song of an entire menagerie!

The next time you're in Australia and hear a strange sound in the forest, listen carefully. You could be witnessing an amazing performance by a lyrebird! These birds are living proof that nature will never cease to surprise us.

Fact 96 - Termite Architectures

Have you ever seen those impressive earthen structures that rise from the ground like ancestral towers? These are the termite mounds, true architectural masterpieces created by these little creatures.

Built primarily from saliva, feces, and soil, these mounds can grow up to several meters high. But it's not just their size that's impressive. These structures play an essential role for termites. They regulate temperature and humidity, creating a perfect environment for the colony.

In Australia, for example, termites' magnetic mounds are oriented from north to south to minimize exposure to the scorching sun. This allows termites to maintain a stable internal microclimate. Ingenious, isn't it?

The next time you come across one of these majestic structures, take a moment to admire the genius of nature. Termites, often perceived as simple pests, are in fact real master builders!

Fact 97 - Whitsundays, Heaven on Earth

Have you ever dreamed of a place where the sky mixes with a turquoise sea and the sand is so white that it dazzles? Welcome to the Whitsundays, an Australian archipelago of 74 idyllic islands nestled in the heart of the Great Barrier Reef.

Each island is a treasure waiting to be discovered. One of the most famous is Whitehaven Beach. Its sand, composed of 98% pure silica, is incredibly soft and does not retain heat. It's a magical place where you could spend hours walking barefoot, admiring the gradient of blues of the ocean.

But the Whitsundays aren't just about heavenly beaches. It is also a rich and colorful underwater world. Put on a mask and snorkel, and dive in to discover the wonders of the Great Barrier Reef, home to exceptional marine biodiversity.

If you're looking for a getaway that combines relaxation, natural beauty and adventure, the Whitsundays are your destination. Every moment you spend here will remind you that heaven on earth does exist.

Fact 98 - Bowerbirds, the Artists of Nature

Have you ever heard of birds who play performers to seduce their partners? Bowerbirds, or garden birds, native to Australia, are exactly that: decorating maestros.

To impress females, the male builds a structure called a "bower". It is not a simple nest, but rather an elaborate work of art. Using twigs and grasses, he forms a small tunnel that he painstakingly decorates with shiny, colorful objects and sometimes even flowers. Some have a soft spot for blue, others for green.

But the talent of these birds doesn't stop there. In addition to decorating, the male performs an intricate dance and sings to seduce his partner. This show is fascinating to watch, a mixture of creativity and determination.

The next time you're walking around Australia and come across a strange cluster of colorful objects on the ground, stop for a moment. You may be standing in front of the work of a Bowerbird, one of the greatest artists in the animal world.

Fact 99 - Echidnas: Prickly but Cute

You know hedgehogs, don't you? But have you ever heard of echidnas? These spiny creatures, native to Australia, are one of a kind and, despite their spines, incredibly endearing.

Their bodies are covered with quills, similar to those of a hedgehog, which serve as a defense mechanism. When they feel threatened, echidnas curl into a ball, exposing only their sharp spines to any potential predators. But don't let this prickly shell fool you, under these thorns hides a curious and charming animal.

Another amazing fact about them is their diet. Echidnas are insectivores that use their long, sticky tongues to catch ants and termites. Their sturdy claws allow them to efficiently dig into the ground in search of these delicious treats.

So, the next time you go down under, keep an eye out for these prickly little beings. Even though they may seem a little intimidating at first, echidnas are actually gentle animals that are worth getting to know about.

Fact 100 - Torres Strait Islands

Have you ever heard of the Torres Strait Islands? Located between the northern tip of Australia and Papua New Guinea, these islands are home to a mosaic of unique cultures that differ from the Aboriginal traditions of the Australian mainland.

The people of these islands, known as Torres Strait Islanders, have a rich history and traditions of their own. Their dances, songs and storytelling reflect a deep connection with the sea, which plays a central role in their daily lives. For example, the Dhoeri, a traditional wind instrument, produces sounds reminiscent of waves and seabird songs.

The islands themselves are breathtakingly beautiful, with crystal clear waters and impressive marine biodiversity. But what really makes this place special is the warmth and hospitality of its inhabitants. Their sense of community is an example to follow.

So, if you're looking for an off-the-beaten-path destination that's rich in history and culture, consider the Torres Strait Islands. You will discover a world where ancestral traditions and modernity coexist in harmony.

Conclusion

There you have it, dear reader, the journey through the 100 incredible facts about Australia is coming to an end. Through these pages, you have explored the vastness of this continent, its natural wonders, its centuries-old traditions and its modern enigmas. If you hadn't already fallen in love with Australia before starting this book, I hope you are now, because it has so much to offer.

Every fact you have discovered is a testament to the richness and diversity of this faraway land. From its unique animals to its Aboriginal legends, Australia is a mosaic of stories and adventures waiting to be experienced. And even if you now have a better understanding of this country, remember that these 100 facts are just the tip of the iceberg.

I hope that this exploration has inspired you, that it has awakened in you the desire to dive deeper into the mysteries of Australia, and why not, to visit it one day. After all, nothing beats first-hand experience. But in the meantime, keep these stories and discoveries in your heart, and share them with others, because Australia, with its magic and beauty, deserves to be celebrated and known by all.

Marc Dresgui

Quiz

1) Which legendary creature is considered the "Bigfoot of Australia"?

   a) Bunyip
   b) Yowie
   c) Tiddalik
   d) Quinkan

2) Which Australian animal is famous for its ability to mimic a variety of sounds?

   a) Koala
   b) Kookaburra
   c) Lyrebird
   d) Echidna

3) What natural structure are termites known to build?

   a) Underground Tunnels
   b) Caves
   c) Nests in trees
   d) Termite Mounds

4) Who was a famous Australian outlaw?

   a) Ned Kelly
   b) Jack Sparrow
   c) Billy the Kid

d) Jesse James

5) What are the spirits of the Wandjinas in Aboriginal mythology?

a) Sun
b) Wind
c) Rain
d) Earth

6) Where would you be likely to encounter a "Drop Bear"?

a) Desert
b) Reefs
c) Australian Forests
d) Snow-capped mountains

7) The Torres Strait Islands are known for their rich...

a) Marine fauna
b) Culture
c) Mining industry
d) Vineyards

8) What is the Australian expression to describe a laid-back attitude to challenges?

a) "Piece of cake"

b) "Keep calm"

c) "She'll be right"

d) "No worries"

9) Australia is known for its beaches that stretch across the Mediterranean.

a) Hundreds of meters away

b) Miles

c) Dozens of kilometres

d) As far as the eye can see

10) Which of these animals is prickly but considered cute?

a) Wombat

b) Echidna

c) Platypus

d) Tasmanian Devil

11) Bowerbirds are known to be...

a) Fast Runners

b) Deep Divers

c) Melodious Singers

d) Nature Artists

12) In Aboriginal mythology, who is considered the creator of the world?

a) Bunyip
b) Yowie
c) Quinkan
d) Rainbow Serpent

13) The Whitsundays are often described as a...

a) Heaven on Earth
b) Arid Desert
c) Industrial Center
d) High mountain peak

14) In which part of Australia would you find giant sand dunes for adventure?

a) Sydney
b) Lancelin
c) Melbourne
d) Tasmania

15) What is the name of the frog in Aboriginal legend who is said to have drunk all the water?

a) Bob
b) Tiddalik
c) Jumper

d) Ribbit

16) Quinkans are associated with what natural element?

a) Water
b) Fire
c) Rocks
d) Air

17) The black dog is a spirit...

a) Happy
b) Disquieting
c) Protector
d) Amusing

18) Which Australian animal is renowned for its melodious wing beats?

a) Koala
b) Kangaroo
c) Lyrebird
d) Possum

19) Which of these spiders is known to be relatively harmless in Australia?

a) Black Widow

b) Tarantula

c) Funnel Web Spider

d) Huntsman Spider

20) What legendary creature is associated with billabong in Australia?

a) Bunyip

b) Drop Bear

c) Yowie

d) Quinkan

Answers

1) Which legendary creature is considered the "Bigfoot of Australia"?

Correct answer: b)Yowie

2) Which Australian animal is famous for its ability to mimic a variety of sounds?

Correct answer: c)Lyrebird

3) What natural structure are termites known to build?

Correct answer: d)Termite Mounds

4) Who was a famous Australian outlaw?

Correct answer: a)Ned Kelly

5) What are the spirits of the Wandjinas in Aboriginal mythology?

Correct answer: c) Rain

6) Where would you be likely to encounter a "Drop Bear"?

Correct answer: (c)Australian forests

7) The Torres Strait Islands are known for their rich...

Correct answer: (b)Culture

8) What is the Australian expression to describe a laid-back attitude to challenges?

Correct answer: c)"She'll be right"

9) Australia is known for its beaches that stretch across the Mediterranean.

Correct answer: d) As far as the eye can see

10) Which of these animals is prickly but considered cute?

Correct answer: b)Echidna

11) Bowerbirds are known to be...

Correct answer: d)Nature artists

12) In Aboriginal mythology, who is considered the creator of the world?

Correct answer: d)Rainbow Serpent

13) The Whitsundays are often described as a...

Correct answer: a) Heaven on earth

14) In which part of Australia would you find giant sand dunes for adventure?

Correct answer: b)Lancelin

15) What is the name of the frog in Aboriginal legend who is said to have drunk all the water?

Correct answer: b)Tiddalik

16) Quinkans are associated with what natural element?

Correct answer: c)Rocks

17) The black dog is a spirit...

Correct answer: b)Worrying

18) Which Australian animal is renowned for its melodious wing beats?

Correct answer: c)Lyrebird

19) Which of these spiders is known to be relatively harmless in Australia?

Correct answer: d)Huntsman Spider

20) What legendary creature is associated with billabong in Australia?

Correct answer: a)Bunyip

Printed in Great Britain
by Amazon

30805341R10066